A PARENT'S GUIDE
TO
PIANO LESSONS

by James W. Bastien

KJOS WEST, 4382 Jutland Drive, San Diego, California

Published by KJOS WEST

Distributed by Neil A. Kjos, Jr., Publisher
4382 Jutland Drive, San Diego, California 92117

© 1976 KJOS WEST, San Diego, California

International Standard Book Number 0-910842-05-1

Library of Congress Card Number 76-21927

Printed and Bound in the United States of America

ISBN 0-910842-05-1

PREFACE

Today's busy parents are bombarded with numerous parental duties and responsibilities. Psychologists and child specialists have written extensively on the subject. Although books on parenthood provide practical suggestions for child raising, little information is included on music study. In fact, few books exist to help answer questions parents may have concerning music lessons.

My purpose in writing *A Parent's Guide to Piano Lessons* is to offer suggestions to parents who are about to start their child on piano lessons, as well as to discuss problems which might be encountered during the first few years of study.

As a parent, your challenge is to help your child get as much out of piano lessons as possible. The aim of this book is to help you meet this challenge.

James W. Bastien

Note: For literary purposes *your child* often is referred to as *he*. This should not imply that there are more boys taking lessons than girls; in fact, quite the contrary is true.

CONTENTS

ONE   **First Considerations** 7

TWO   **Selecting a Teacher** 17

THREE   **Selecting a Piano** 25

FOUR   **Helping Your Beginner** 35

FIVE   **Practice Suggestions** 44

SIX   **Recitals, Contests, Festivals and Auditions** 51

Appendix A   **Brief Outline of Music Facts** 57

Appendix B   **Brief Dictionary of Musical Terms** 67

Appendix C   **Brief Reference Listing** 70

ONE

FIRST CONSIDERATIONS

Each year thousands of youngsters begin piano lessons. Most children love music and are delighted at the prospect of making music themselves. Music is an enriching element in everyone's life and can touch an individual in a special way. However, it is helpful to consider some basic questions before jumping headlong into lessons. The answers to these questions will be useful in determining the feasibility of starting your child on piano lessons at this time.

How can I tell if my child wants piano lessons?

It is a natural desire for children to want music lessons. Music is all around us—on TV, radio and phonograph. Even Musak is a part of our daily lives. With this constant exposure to music of all kinds, children want to make music themselves. School band and orchestra programs provide outlets for self-made music on a variety of instruments, but when it comes to private instruction, piano lessons come to mind first.

According to the American Music Conference (an organization of instrument manufacturers, music publishers and music merchants) 37,000,000 Americans now play musical instruments. A survey done by this organization in 1972 revealed that 26.3% of all amateur musicians were taking private lessons. Of those taking private instruction, an amazing 60% were taking *piano lessons.*[1]

Reader's Digest had an interesting article entitled "What Every Parent Needs to Know About Music Lessons" which began by saying: "Sometime in most every parent's life he hears his child saying, 'I want to learn a musical instrument' (half of all youngsters begin to play something.)"[2]

If your child tells you he wants to take piano lessons, take him seriously. He probably has a friend or an older brother or sister who is taking lessons, and he is intrigued by what he hears them playing.

---

[1]According to this survey even more children took private piano lessons than guitar lessons; instruction in guitar accounted for only 15% of those taking private lessons.

[2]Quoted with permission from the August 1973 *Reader's Digest*. Condensed from the *Baltimore Sunday Sun.* ® Copyright 1973 by the Reader's Digest Association, Inc.

Direct communication from the *child* should be given prime consideration. A mother reported that at the age of four her little girl marched across the street to the home of a piano teacher and announced that she had come to take her "lesson." She opened the book she brought and exclaimed, "I would like to play 'Little Orphan Annie.'" The teacher listened patiently to the child's rendition, then promptly called the girl's mother and lessons were started. This is an extreme case, but the child really wanted to begin lessons; this initial step by the child eventually led to a successful career in music.

Another indication of a child's interest in music may be evidenced by a fascination with the piano. If you have a piano in your home, observe how your child relates to it. If friends call to inform you that your child loves to "play" their piano, give your child's interest serious thought. All children are tempted to "bang" on the piano at random. However, a child with real interest in music may attempt to pick out simple melodies he has heard.

Does your child receive satisfaction from learning new things? In general, is he eager to learn? Any child can learn to play the piano to some degree, but a child who is highly motivated to learn will make substantial progress over another child who would rather be playing or watching TV.

With a little observation and interest evaluation you can determine if your child really wants piano lessons. Careful consideration of beginning factors will contribute to success in music.

CHECKLIST

How can I tell if my child wants piano lessons?

- *child asks for lessons*
- *he is fascinated with the piano*
- *he likes to learn*

Is the piano a good choice for my child's first instrument?

The piano is often called the *complete musical instrument.* It is possible to experience all elements of music on the piano: melody, rhythm and harmony. Piano study provides the beginner with basic music facts such as notation in *both* clefs, counting time and music theory. In addition, the beginner may learn to improvise and play by ear. The foundation received on the piano at the beginning of music study will serve the child in any musical direction he chooses to pursue, whether or not he continues the piano. Thus, a year or two of piano study provides an ideal preparation for later study of other musical instruments.

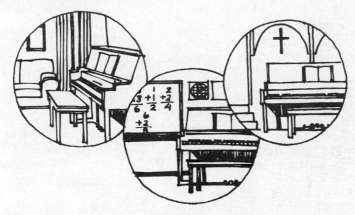

The piano is readily accessible. It is found in homes, school classrooms, churches and many other places. The youngster who can play a piano solo or accompany a group in singing is an instant hit. Unlike other instrumentalists, the pianist needs no accompanist. He can provide complete music for others to enjoy in many settings.

Compared to many other instruments, the piano is easy to learn to play. On the violin (and other string instruments) the correct pitch must be made with the left hand on the fingerboard. On the French horn (and other wind instruments) the correct pitch must be made with the lips. Both these processes take a good deal of time and effort to produce music which is "easily" listened to. However, on the piano ready-made pitches can be produced by merely pressing down the keys. Therefore, a child can make music in a much shorter time on the piano than on most other instruments.

One advantage of piano study is that skills learned can be transferred later to other keyboard instruments. This factor is especially important for those who want to play the organ for church or play an electronic piano in a rock group.

Throughout life the piano is an excellent source of pleasure. Because the piano is both a solo and an accompanying instrument, enjoyment may come from both solitary music-making and participating with others.

If you have musician friends, other than pianists, ask their opinion on what instrument to study *first*. The majority will suggest the piano. The piano is basic. It provides an ideal background for any musical pursuit.

CHECKLIST

Is the piano a good choice for my child's first instrument?

- *the piano is a complete musical instrument*
- *it is accessible*
- *it is easy to learn*
- *it is basic*

How can I tell if my child has musical talent?

Merriam-Webster defines talent as "the abilities, powers, and gifts bestowed upon man (natural endowments), thought of as a divine trait." For example, Mozart evidenced amazing talent at the age of six; his ability to play and compose sophisticated pieces was quite miraculous, and he was exhibited all over Europe as a child prodigy! This kind of musical talent is given to a precious few. Special talent (innate ability) such as this is, in all probability, an inherited trait. To what extent, however, is not known.

For children with no previous musical training, talent is almost impossible to assess. Indeed, few authorities can agree on what talent is. Two important indications, however, are an accurate sense of pitch and a natural sense of rhythm. Does your child sing "in tune"? Does he "feel" music rhythmically? Does your child try to pick out one-finger melodies on a piano? If he can do this much on his own, he definitely shows signs of talent.

CHECKLIST

How can I tell if my child has musical talent?

- *child has an accurate sense of pitch*
- *he has a natural sense of rhythm*

Is musical talent important?

The average child may not evidence a natural ability for the piano up to this point. You may exclaim, "That's for sure, our child is no Mozart!" Let me encourage you further; most children studying the piano show little musical ability prior to beginning lessons. For the most part, they are learning to play the piano as an extension of the learning process, as an avocation, not a profession. Therefore, "unusual" signs of talent such as *perfect pitch* (the ability to identify tones heard with exactness), and the ability to *play by ear* with no previous musical training are rarities which are not at all prerequisites for piano lessons.

Kathy was a bright little girl who practiced an hour a day. Her teacher was amazed at what she accomplished with seemingly very little musical ability. Kathy said repeatedly, "I love my pieces, and I love to come to my lessons." More than talent, Kathy had desire and motivation and did consistently good work.

Musical talent is often deceptive. No one can draw hasty conclusions about who is and who is not musically gifted. Senses of pitch and rhythm are usually skills developed over a period of time. Slow learners may become late bloomers; children who "can't carry a tune" may develop vocal skills later; a beginner who is having rhythm problems because of hand coordination may become much more adept with practice. There are no hard and fast rules when it comes to talent.

Perhaps talent will manifest itself in another instrument. Not all children are suited solely for piano study. A child who is musically talented may not appear to be talented at the piano, because he is studying the *wrong* instrument for him. Sometimes experimentation with other instruments will reveal talent not immediately obvious.

Sometimes talent can even work against its possessor. Frequently a very talented child finds music so easy that he puts forth less and less effort and may develop sloppy habits. Without application, talent may go to waste.

Take heart, dear parent. Talent is usually 90% application and 10% inspiration. If piano teachers taught only "God-given talents," they would have few (if any) students! If your child is interested in music generally, and in the piano specifically, he can learn to play with or without possessing any special, innate ability.

CHECKLIST

Is musical talent important?

- *desire and motivation come first*
- *application is 90% of talent*

Will my child stick with it?

Although you are pleased that your child is interested in taking lessons, you may wonder: Will he like it? Will he practice? Are we getting into something which is difficult to get out of? Will the money spent on the piano and lessons go down the drain? Will he stick with it?

While success or failure cannot be predicted, most beginners make it through a two-year lesson period. It is at this point that some of them begin to weaken. Some show interest in another instrument, and others find demands of homework and extracurricular activities increasing to the point where practice time is in short supply.

In the beginning a piano dealer can put your mind at ease by renting a piano to you for several months. This arrangement gets the beginner started at a modest cost. Neither you nor your child need feel any burden of guilt if for some reason your child discovers that the piano is not for him.

Usually beginners are intrigued with lessons, and the majority will stick with it. However, it is not the end of the world if your child does not "take" to piano lessons. Encourage, prod and praise, but if you find yourself in a frustrating, tense, losing situation, let him discontinue lessons. But leave the door open. Tell him: "If you don't enjoy it, let's drop it for now; perhaps you will come back to it later." It's not uncommon to see a youngster drop lessons, start again later, take more interest and be successful. At worst, if your child insists on stopping lessons, don't make him feel guilty about it by exclaiming: "I bought this expensive piano for you. You have no appreciation for what I'm trying to do for you. Think how much money you have cost me!"

You can help your child through the beginning stages of lessons by setting realistic goals and offering specific rewards for achieving them. Show interest in your child's progress by listening to lesson assignments and giving encouragement and praise where possible. Under the guidance of a sympathetic teacher the majority will enjoy their lessons, will look forward to receiving new materials and will stick with it.[3]

CHECKLIST

Will my child stick with it?

- *most beginners study for two years*
- *the beginner needs your encouragement and praise*
- *the beginner should not be forced to continue*

What is the best age to start piano lessons?

Beginning piano instruction usually is given to children varying in age from about seven to eleven years old. The age of beginners varies for a number of reasons: children request lessons at different ages; parents purchase pianos at varying times; and parents and teachers have diverse opinions regarding an appropriate beginning age.

Most authorities agree that a child should have completed at least one year of elementary school before he begins piano lessons. The child should be able to *read* the directions in his first piano book. Some teachers prefer to wait until a child is in the third or fourth grade: "For private lessons, which imply some note-reading and individual follow-through from the start, most teachers stake the threshold at the third grade (and not earlier than the second)

---

[3]For a useful, general appraisal of child-parent problems regarding music lessons, read *Between Parent and Child* by Dr. Haim G. Ginott (The Macmillan Company, 1965), pp. 82-85.

when children have some competence in reading words."[4] The exception to starting lessons at the age of seven (second grade) may be those who began first grade when they were only five years old. Those children usually need an additional year of schooling before taking on piano lessons.

The main consideration for an optimum beginning age is a *readiness* level which varies from child to child. Can your child read fairly easily? Can he concentrate for a period of time? Is school work fairly easy for him? Does he have good coordination of his small muscles?[5] If your realistic answer is "no" to any of these questions, you might consider starting your child on piano lessons at a later time. However, a spontaneous interest may indicate that your child has reached the best time to start lessons. Moreover, experience has shown that once this time has passed, it may be lost forever. Gifted children especially benefit from an early beginning. The later your child starts, the more difficult it will be to avoid conflicts of homework and extracurricular activities. However, it is never too late to start; this fact is proven by a vast number of teenagers and adults beginning lessons.

Special consideration must be given here to very young beginners: four-, five-, and six-year-olds. Head Start programs and TV programs such as *Sesame Street* have taught us the advantage of early learning. Introductory structured learning may aid the preschool child in understanding basic concepts and simple reasoning processes. Early music lessons, in addition to teaching purely musical facts, will train the child in principles of reasoning which may be carried over into other learning experiences. Also, developmental

[4]Robert W. Dumm, "Piano Lessons?—three big questions first." Reprinted by permission from *The Christian Monitor.* © Copyright 1966 The Christian Science Publishing Society. All rights reserved.

[5]Boys may have more difficulty with coordination of small muscles than girls at a young age. In some instances more success is achieved starting boys on lessons at a later time.

sensory-motor skills assimilated through piano study will generally aid the child in coordination of small and large muscles.

If your child shows genuine interest in music at an early age, seek a teacher who has had experience teaching this age group; the average piano teacher may not be proficient in the teaching of young children. If your child begins lessons at an early age, be prepared to work with him, because he probably will not be able to read words. Preschool piano is a special area which is beginning to grow rapidly. An increasing number of teachers are offering this instruction, and new materials are constantly being developed for young children.

A child should begin formal instruction *only* when he is able to absorb instruction and practice on a regular basis. The basic requirements for a child to understand music are the ability to reason and the desire to learn. Until your child reaches a readiness age for piano instruction, you can cultivate an awareness of music by exposing your child to music of all kinds. You can encourage music experimentation through singing, and you can help to develop rhythmic awareness and basic coordination through movement or dance. A rich musical home background will set the stage for formal music instruction when your child is ready for it.

CHECKLIST

What is the best age to start piano lessons?

- *when a child is between 7 and 11 years old*
- *after he can read*
- *when he reaches his readiness level*

What is the purpose and goal of piano lessons?

Music is a vital part of human life. In every culture some form of music-making is included, from the most primitive society to the most advanced. Music is a language which transcends speech and is understood the world over.

Piano lessons have become standard fare as an acceptable social activity and as a part of general childhood education. Regardless of special talent, millions of students are engaged in the pursuit of musical instruction as an *extension* of the general learning process. It is usually not the intent or purpose of those studying to become professional musicians. Rather, for the majority, the general philosophy is that music study will develop a special skill which will *enrich* and *broaden* their lives. Music becomes a satisfying experience that gives direction to the basic needs of self-expression, an appreciation for beauty and an outlet for emotional release.

In most school systems music and art have some place in the

over-all curriculum. Unfortunately, economic considerations lead to inconsistent application of music and art programs, and these two special areas are often eliminated because they are considered "frills." They are not part of the three R's, so they are the first to be cut and the last to be reinstated. This misconception of the arts as secondary in relation to the school curriculum is most unfortunate. It robs youngsters of opportunities to participate in activities other than basic core courses. To help fill this gap, piano lessons can be a welcome activity for many children. Through piano study they will be exposed to music and will not be left with a musical void.

Compared to general school work, the rewards of piano lessons touch the child in a special way. When a youngster brings home his report card and shows his grades, that is the end of the matter. But when a new piece is learned, he can share this with his family and contribute to the family's pleasure.

Piano lessons can be a significant part of your child's development, whether he studies for two years or for ten. Even a brief encounter with lessons can provide him with a rudimentary understanding of music which will enable him to appreciate musical ability in others and to appreciate music in general. You should understand that the rewards of piano lessons will far exceed the ability to play well. Just as every child can study mathematics without expecting to become another Einstein, the piano can be studied without each child expecting to become another Van Cliburn. A musical background will enrich each person and can remain a lifelong source of personal enjoyment and fulfillment.

CHECKLIST

What is the purpose and goal of piano lessons?

- *to enrich and broaden a child's experience*
- *to add to his basic core courses*
- *to develop his appreciation for music*

TWO

SELECTING A TEACHER

The piano teacher who has an enthusiasm for music, a liking for children and a desire to teach can inspire and motivate the student and stimulate his interest and curiosity in music. In this regard, a skilled teacher is one who knows more than the notes; he is an effective communicator who can impart knowledge and cause others to learn. It is well worth the time and effort to find a teacher with these attributes.

What elements make a good teacher?

Your child will be working with a piano teacher for at least thirty minutes a week for nine months each year (longer, if summer lessons are taken). The piano teacher exerts considerable influence over your child, and you want to make sure the association is pleasant and beneficial. Considering this, you want the *best* teacher for your child, even if the child is a beginner!

Is the best teacher the most expensive one in the community? Is the best teacher a concert pianist? Is the best teacher young or old, male or female, lax or stern? Many questions such as these are raised by parents. Moreover, the "best" teacher may not be right for every child. Some teachers prefer working with advanced students, others specialize in teaching beginners.

Teachers vary in training and proficiency. Some have college music degrees, others have had only a few years of training; some are professional artists who perform regularly, while others can scarcely play at all and never perform. Credentials, such as degrees, performance background or professional certification, are important criteria in determining standards. However, training and background alone will not assure competent teaching. Other significant factors are the teacher's personality, experience, interest in teaching and "track record."

Is it important for a teacher to have a music degree? First, it is an indication that the individual has a competent musical background and should be qualified to teach. However, even a doctorate in music won't guarantee that a person is a *good* teacher. As a parent, you have witnessed good and bad teachers working with your child at school. These teachers usually are certified to teach, but there is a great variance in approaches and the results achieved. Realistically, some people are more adept at teaching than others. Thus, although a degree or certification does indicate background and subject knowledge, any or all of these qualifications do not guarantee success in teaching.

Is it important for a teacher to be a performer? Paradoxically, you can't judge a teacher by his ability to play the piano. This is particularly true for the teacher whose specialty is teaching beginners. For success in this area, patience, understanding, warmth in approach, and a familiarity with beginning teaching methods and techniques are most important. If a gifted teacher is working near you, you will hear of it from delighted parents of delighted children. If there is a subtle choice between teachers, "put personality before performance, enthusiasm for music and love for children before credentials. Dreariness may mask itself with method, and dislike for teaching may hide behind a 'big name.' "[6]

A public performer does exhibit professionalism which can be assessed by fellow musicians and critics. Performance prowess gives you confidence that the person is a professional who knows his business. However, a public performer or concert artist is not necessarily a sympathetic teacher. In fact, he may not like teaching children at all, but he may have to teach to support himself. Bess Myerson hits the nail on the head by stating: "Parents must choose teachers who can bring understanding and warmth to children. It is not enough that a teacher be a brilliant technician or a martinet who scowls at clinkers and thanks only God and himself when a passage is well played. That kind of teacher may 'preserve' his art and kill his students' love for music forever."[7]

Once lessons have commenced you can evaluate your child's relationship with the teacher: Is he eager to go to lessons? Does he

---

[6]Robert W. Dumm, "Piano Lessons?—three big questions first." Reprinted by permission from *The Christian Science Monitor.* © Copyright 1966 The Christian Science Publishing Society. All rights reserved.

[7]Bess Myerson, "My Mother, My Piano—And Me." Reprinted courtesy of *Redbook Magazine*, June 1974 issue.

have a good attitude upon returning from lessons? Unfortunately, these factors cannot be assessed until lessons begin.

An ideal piano teacher would be one who can (or could) perform, has had experience teaching children, has a good personality and likes to teach. Usually, in most cities there are a number of teachers who possess this rich background. If you locate a teacher who has qualities such as a genuine love and understanding of music, imagination, enthusiasm, patience, sincerity and dedication, and a sense of humor, you probably will have selected an excellent beginning teacher.

CHECKLIST

What elements make a good teacher?

- *pleasant personality*
- *dedication*
- *experience*
- *teaching expertise*

How important is a good beginning teacher?

A first grade teacher has most of the responsibility for teaching your child to read. Much of what a child is able to accomplish in school is dependent on how well he can read. Thus, the teaching of correct beginning reading habits is very important. Likewise, a "beginning" piano teacher must impart all basic music information to your child, such as beginning technical skills, notation, rhythm, and sight-reading habits. Much of what your child will be able to accomplish in music will be based on a solid foundation in beginning fundamentals. In most cases the beginning years are critical, because first impressions, good or bad, persist.

Don't be misled into judging teachers by the *level* of students they teach. For example, a university professor who teaches advanced college students is often thought to be "better" than a teacher who specializes in working with beginners. This definitely is not true. Teaching beginners is one of the most demanding tasks in the music profession. Good "beginning" teachers make an important musical contribution to the community, and they are deserving of more recognition than they often receive.

CHECKLIST

How important is a good beginning teacher?

- *beginning years are critical to later accomplishments*
- *"beginning" teachers can do much to stimulate a child's lasting interest in music*

How do I find the right teacher?

There are a number of sources available to help you locate a teacher. First, there is word-of-mouth awareness. You may hear about an outstanding teacher from your friends or from your children's friends. Attend a recital given by this teacher's pupils; you will be able to make a judgment about the quality of work this teacher does. The name of a teacher with a good teaching reputation will stand out in the community.

Second, if you have a college or university music department in your area, check with them for recommendations. The music department may even have a *preparatory department* which specializes in teaching pre-college students. In such a situation students of the college often teach children as part of their training. The lessons usually are of good quality and instruction is well-supervised and controlled. Lessons are given on the campus with the approval of the college.

Third, a music store which specializes in the sale of pianos can be of great help in locating a teacher. The piano salesman knows area teachers, and he can make helpful suggestions.

Fourth, school teachers, especially music specialists, are good sources of information. In some cases, lessons are given in the schools. The piano teacher is either employed by the school system or an outside teacher comes to the school to give lessons.

Fifth, you can inquire about piano instruction from your church organist or choir director. Often the organist gives piano lessons himself; if not, he can recommend a teacher.

You can easily find a teacher for your child if you investigate any or all of these sources. However, some teachers have more requests for lessons than they can handle, and prospective students are put on a waiting list.

The next step is to make contact with one or more teachers. Information, such as lesson fees and what type of program is offered (private or group instruction, theory lessons, etc.), can easily be obtained on the phone.[8]

CHECKLIST

How do I find the right teacher?

- *by word-of-mouth*
- *through a college or university*
- *at a music store*
- *from a school music specialist or church musician*

---

[8]For an insight into lesson fees (and music lessons in general), see "Music Lessons Without the Blues" by Ralph Tyler in *Money* magazine (September, 1974).

Is an interview necessary?

Although information can be given on the phone, there is no substitute for personal contact. An interview is recommended. Make an appointment for an interview with the teacher. Bring your child to the interview. Let the teacher talk to your child *alone* for some of the interview time. Parents have a way of talking *for* their child; the teacher needs to know your child's views concerning lessons (maybe your child doesn't want to take lessons), and your child can talk candidly if you're not there.

Generally, the teacher will explain the type of program offered and perhaps outline objectives. The teaching program offered may be quite different from the one with which you are familiar, and the interview should be used to clarify any misgivings that you or your child might have. For example, your child may not realize that he will be required to practice a certain amount each day, and that there should be time in his schedule for this. He may be equating piano lessons with other activities, such as ballet, gymnastics or swimming, for which practice at home may not be required. In short, the three parties (child, parent and teacher) need to understand each other. Both the child and parent should know exactly what they are getting into *before* enrolling for lessons.

From the interview you can get an indication of your child's reaction to the teacher. Your child is the one taking lessons. You want to make certain the association is mutually agreeable. Ask your child his opinion. Children usually are forthright and honest. If your child has misgivings, he will probably tell you. Your instinct will guide you. If you feel that this teacher is not right for your child, look elsewhere. Don't begin lessons with a teacher merely for convenience. Even though the teacher lives in the same block, he may not be the *right* teacher for your child. Find the teacher who will turn your child on to music, even if you have to drive across town!

CHECKLIST

Is an interview necessary?

- *recommended for your appraisal of the teacher*
- *recommended for the teacher's appraisal of your child*
- *recommended for your child's reaction to the teacher*

Should my child take private or group lessons?

Although group lessons are now offered, relatively few teachers are engaged in group instruction. Most teachers offer private lessons. There are merits in both systems. Actually, it is the *teacher* who is the determining factor in successful teaching, not the situation.

The rewards of personal attention received in private lessons cannot be denied; this is especially true for more advanced students. However, for beginners (young ones especially) the psychological benefits of participating with others is an enjoyable social experience which often provides additional motivation beyond what the teacher can offer. Frequently group lessons are augmented by private or semiprivate lessons. In this way attention can be given to both individual and group needs.

One of the most important aspects of group lessons, if taught by a skillful teacher, is an exposure to more than just piano playing. Items, such as theory instruction, ear training, ensemble work, sight-reading, and drills in music fundamentals, usually are offered in class lessons. In addition, children who have some group experience learn to overcome their shyness about performing for others.

Private or group, *results* are what count. Remember, the quality of instruction offered is dependent on the teacher, not necessarily on the teaching situation.

CHECKLIST

Should my child take private or group lessons?

- *success of private or group instruction depends on the effectiveness of the teacher*
- *group instruction provides the benefit of participation with others*
- *group instruction offers exposure to more than just piano playing*

THREE

SELECTING A PIANO

The process of purchasing a piano is much like buying an appliance, furniture or an automobile. Many choices are available from a wide selection ranging from small, inexpensive pianos to large, expensive ones. However, selecting a piano does not have to be a traumatic experience. Ask for suggestions from your piano teacher, your piano teacher's tuner, from school and church musicians, and from friends and acquaintances. Look in the phone directory for dealer listings. Visit several music stores before coming to a decision.

Should I rent or purchase a piano?

First, it may be wise to wait to rent or purchase a piano until *after* interviewing a teacher (or teachers), because the teacher's judgment may be that your child is not yet ready for lessons, and that he should be started later. However, if you have been given the "green light" to begin lessons, you *must* have a piano for your child's practice. It will not suffice for your child to have to practice at a neighbor's or relative's home, or in a school or church room. Don't make the mistake of beginning lessons until you have a piano at *home!*

Lisa was enthusiastic about beginning piano lessons and was determined to start even though she had to practice on her neighbor's piano. There were many conflicts between her practice schedule and her neighbor's activities which frequently resulted in no practice. Lisa often felt guilty about coming to her lessons unprepared.

If money is a primary factor in deciding whether to start lessons now or later, by all means rent. By renting a piano in the beginning, you can get your child started at a minimal cost. Compare rental prices at several music stores, because rental prices vary between dealers.

If you purchase a piano you will be making a sizeable investment. Shop around and select carefully. You may find that purchasing a piano will really "turn on" your child. Pride of ownership can work wonders. Owning a piano could unlock the door to your child's musical talents.

CHECKLIST

Should I rent or purchase a piano?

- *wait until after the interview*
- *if money's a factor, rent*
- *if you purchase, select carefully*

What types of pianos are available?

Briefly, there are four basic types of pianos. From smallest to largest, pianos are named *spinet, console, studio* (sometimes referred to as an upright) and *grand*. The first three are *vertical* shaped pianos (upright pianos). Grand pianos are *horizontal* in shape.

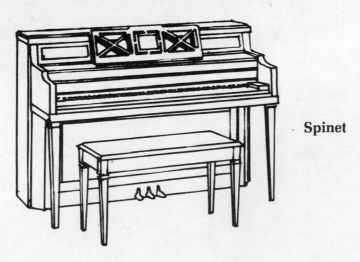

Spinet

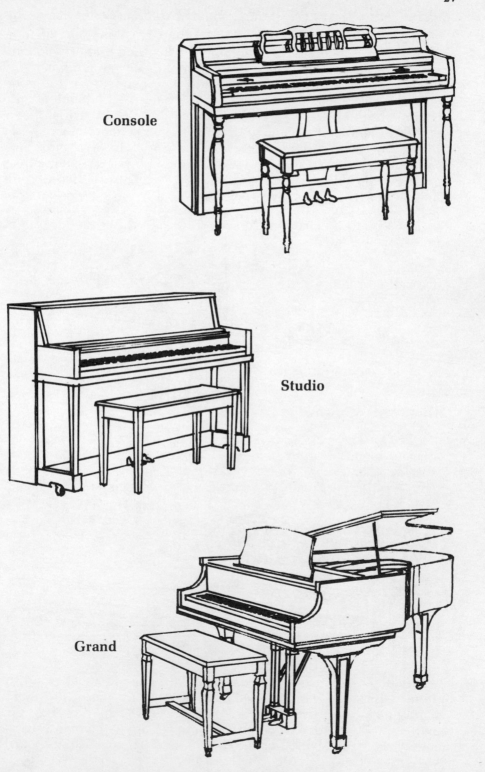

Console

Studio

Grand

What similarities or differences are found among pianos?

The *action* of all pianos is similar. In vertical pianos the *hammer* strikes the *strings,* which are upright; in grand pianos, the hammer strikes the strings, which are horizontal. The action has many moving parts. The touch of the piano is dependent on the good working order (regulation) of the piano's action. The touch should be firm, not too loose. If a child practices on a piano which has a very loose action, he will have trouble adjusting to actions of other pianos. The spinet has an *indirect-blow* action. It has two more separating levers per key than a console, studio or grand piano, whose action is referred to as a *direct-blow* action. Thus, the spinet has more moving parts to go awry and may tend to have a loose action.

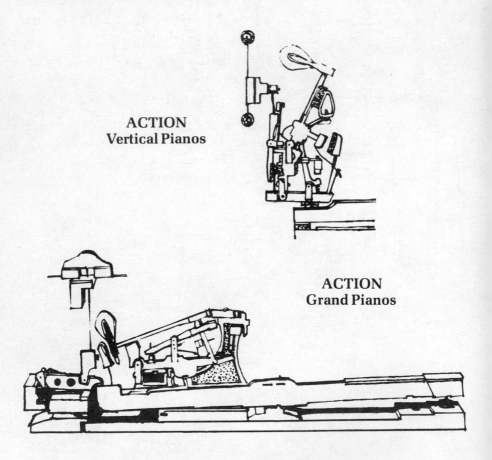

ACTION
Vertical Pianos

ACTION
Grand Pianos

In all pianos there is a *soundboard* (the "loud speaker" of the piano) which is visible at the back of vertical pianos and inside grand pianos. The soundboard is largely responsible for determining the quality of tone by amplifying the sound made by the strings as they are struck by felt-covered hammers. The best soundboards are made of straight-grained spruce and are varnished carefully. A good soundboard is laminated with about four thin sheets of spruce glued together—more sheets indicate better quality. The spinet has a 36-inch soundboard; the console and studio pianos have at least a 40-inch soundboard. On grands the soundboards go up to as much as 8 feet, 11 inches. Generally, a bigger piano has a bigger sound.

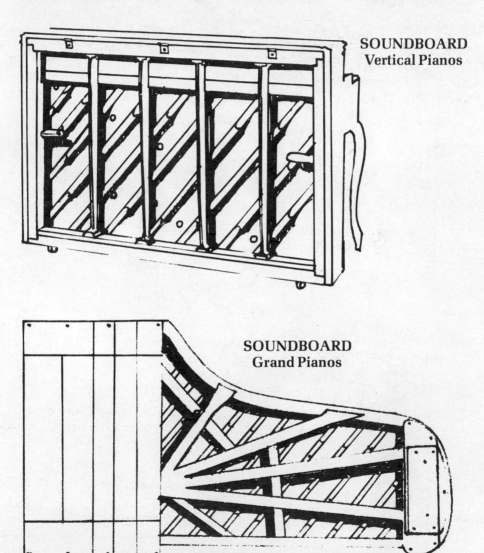

SOUNDBOARD
Vertical Pianos

SOUNDBOARD
Grand Pianos

The soundboard runs the length of the *harp* (a metal plate which holds the strings) and goes into the *pin block*, which is visible when the tops of vertical pianos are lifted and is visible at the front of grand pianos. A good pin block should be made of two or three thicknesses of laminated maple glued together. The *pins* of the piano must be held firmly in place in the pin block for the piano to stay in tune.

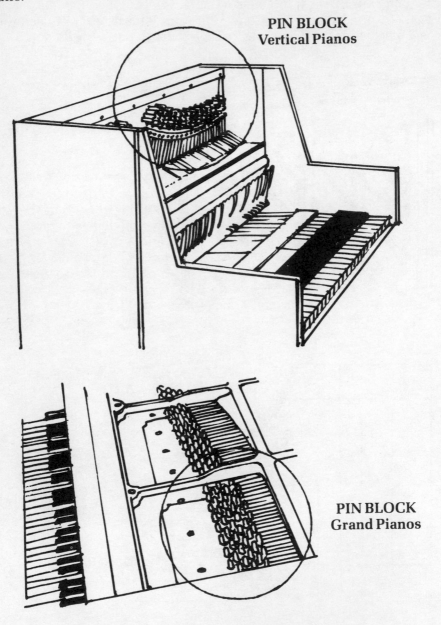

PIN BLOCK
Vertical Pianos

PIN BLOCK
Grand Pianos

Most pianos have at least two pedals, some pianos have three. The pedal on the right is called the *sustaining pedal*. When this pedal is depressed, all the dampers of the strings are raised to allow them to vibrate freely. The pedal on the left is called the *soft pedal*.

PEDALS

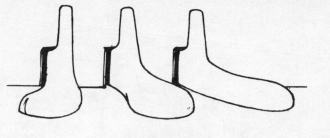

Soft Pedal   **Sostenuto Pedal**   **Sustaining Pedal**

Depressing this pedal moves the hammers closer to the strings on vertical pianos, thus striking from less distance to produce a softer sound. On grands, the keyboard shifts to the right when the soft pedal is depressed, thus the hammers hit fewer strings to produce a softer sound. The center pedal (if there is one) is called a *sostenuto pedal*. Its function is to sustain one or more isolated tones. The correct function of this pedal is somewhat limited on most vertical pianos. An advanced pianist needs all three pedals. Basically, a beginner needs just the sustaining pedal.

CHECKLIST

What similarities or differences are found among pianos?

- *action of all pianos is similar*
- *touch varies (loose to firm)*
- *tone is dependent on length of strings and soundboard*

How much will a piano cost?

For an estimate of what you can expect to spend for a good new piano, here are some *general* price ranges: for a spinet, about $1,200; for consoles, about $1,300 to $1,500; for studio pianos, about $1,800 to $3,000; for a grand, about $3,700 and up. These are approximate prices which are apt to rise with inflation.

Most new, brand-name pianos carry a ten-year guarantee. Unlike a car which wears out and depreciates quickly, a piano will last a lifetime if given proper care and may even appreciate in value. Although an expensive purchase, a good piano should be worth approximately 80% of its original purchase price throughout its lifetime. (This may become apparent after a search has been made for a good used piano!)

How much you pay for a piano depends in part on how well it's made and whether it is a brand name such as Baldwin, Cable-Nelson, Chickering, Everett, Hammond, Kawai, Kimball, Knabe, Mason-Hamlin, Sohmer, Steinway, Story and Clark, Wurlitzer,

Yamaha, and others. What kind of a cabinet you select also influences the price of the piano. Piano cabinets are available in cherry, walnut, oak, formica, ebony or other finishes. Cabinet styles can be selected to match your room, such as French Provincial, Early American, American Traditional, Italian Provincial or Contemporary. Both expensive wood finishes and furniture styles are lovely to look at, but they have little effect on the tone and touch of the piano.

You may have a problem deciding which make of piano to buy. Each piano salesman will tell you the merits of the brand he is selling, just like a car salesman. When buying a car, any make in good working order will go from one place to another, whether it's a Honda or a Rolls Royce; your choice depends on the style in which you would like to ride. The same is true of pianos; all will produce music. Therefore, listen to piano salesmen, read the brochures they give you, try various pianos, and then try to select the size (color, finish, style, etc.) and brand which you think will best suit your needs. Because many vertical pianos are about the same size, they sound much alike. Remember, tone quality is largely dependent on the size of the soundboard and the length of the strings.

If you can't decide for yourself which piano to purchase, you can request help from your piano teacher, musician friend or from a piano tuner. Buying a piano is much like buying anything else—you get what you pay for.

CHECKLIST

How much will a piano cost?

• *depends on size, finish and brand name*

What about a used piano?

Since pianos last a long time, a used piano may be a good choice, especially if you are on a tight budget. A good piano technician (tuner) can re-do an old piano into a fine instrument. He can overhaul the action by putting new felts and other parts where necessary. He can re-string the piano, if necessary. Even the finish of the case and keys on the keyboard can be made to look like new. Thus, often for less money, a used piano is a wise purchase. The quality of a used piano is often dependent on the work it received from a competent piano technician. Again, if you are uncertain about the used piano you would like to buy, ask your piano teacher, a musician friend or another piano tuner (one other than the technician who worked on the piano).

CHECKLIST

What about a used piano?

- *a good choice if budget is tight*
- *a good investment if well-overhauled*

What about an electronic piano?

The electronic piano came into being about the late 1940's. It is the current featured "star performer" in rock groups along with the electric guitar. For someone on the move, it has the advantage of being lightweight and usually needs no tuning. Makes such as Wurlitzer and Fender Rhodes produce tones by hammers striking metal reeds instead of strings. The Baldwin Electropiano has strings like an acoustic piano (regular piano), and it must be tuned. All electronic pianos use an amplifier to expand the sound. All electronic pianos also have an earphone jack, which is an added feature if causing noise is a problem where you live (apartment, trailer, houseboat, etc.)

Electronic pianos come with 64, 73 or 88 keys. Most of them take up less space than vertical acoustic pianos. The touch mechanism varies from mediocre to fair on most electronic pianos. Electronic pianos are used most often in classroom situations for group piano instruction. They are not ideal practice pianos, but they do have advantages such as small size and portability; most of them do not need tuning; they may be played "silently" (with headphones); and they may possibly be less expensive than acoustic pianos.

CHECKLIST

What about an electronic piano?

* *an electronic piano is smaller and portable*
* *it can be played "silently"*
* *it is possibly less expensive*

Where should the piano be placed?

Years ago the piano was placed in the parlor to make sure visitors would be aware of the family's cultural achievements. Today, the most popular choice for the location is the living room or the family room.

The choice of location should be determined by the room which would be the most ideal for practice. Put the piano in a room where your child can study and concentrate in relative peace and quiet. He will be able to accomplish more in this atmosphere than one in which other children are running through the room, the dog is barking or the TV is blaring. If the TV is in the living room, then it is best to avoid conflicts by putting the piano in the family room. If the piano is used exclusively for a child's music lessons, an ideal location is his bedroom where he can practice when he wants in a setting conducive to study and concentration.

CHECKLIST

Where should the piano be placed?

* *in a quiet place*
* *in a room away from family activity*
* *in a room conducive to concentration*

FOUR

HELPING YOUR BEGINNER

Your responsibility as a parent does not end once lessons begin, even though it's your child who is taking lessons, not you. Especially in the beginning, your help is needed to get piano study started in an *organized* manner so that your child will form correct habits which will equip him to continue more on his own.

What can I do to help make lessons go smoothly?

Keep the appointment. When you arrange for a lesson time you are, in effect, buying a specific time from the teacher each week. You are responsible for getting your child to his lesson time promptly. Therefore, write down the lesson time (or times), and post it where it will be seen easily (on the refrigerator, for example).

Notify the teacher of cancellations. Missed lessons cause scheduling problems for teachers. Notify the teacher in *advance* if your child has to miss a lesson so a make-up lesson can be arranged. (Sometimes it is possible to switch lesson times with another student.) If not reported in advance, some teachers do not make up lessons, and they charge for the time missed. Learn what your teacher's

policy is regarding missed lessons. In any case, don't leave the teacher waiting, wondering what happened to your child. Call if your child has to be absent so the teacher can make other arrangements to use that time slot.

Make sure your child arrives at his lesson with all materials. Occasionally a student will come to his lesson with no music; or he may arrive with the wrong music. It is frustrating for the teacher if a lesson has to be improvised because of nonexistent or incorrect materials. Therefore, check to see if your child has his music before going to his lesson. And check to see that he has the *correct* music. (Mix-ups in music often happen in a family where more than one child is taking lessons.) Your teacher will be grateful if you are conscientious in checking materials!

Pay lesson fees promptly. Your teacher should inform you how bills are to be paid. Some teachers charge by the lesson, others

charge by the month. Some teachers send bills home with the student, others send them in the mail. Some teachers charge in advance, others wait and send bills home at the end of the month. Make sure you *understand* which procedure your child's teacher uses and be prepared to pay promptly when fees are due. Sometimes teachers are forced to terminate lessons if bills remain delinquent.

CHECKLIST

What can I do to help make lessons go smoothly?

- *keep the appointment*
- *notify the teacher of cancellations*
- *make sure your child arrives at his lesson with all materials*
- *pay lesson fees promptly*

What materials will be needed?

A music case. Although it is not a requirement of all teachers, a music case is well worth the cost. Your child can keep his music, pencils, workbooks, notebook and any other loose materials all in one place. Things will be less apt to get lost (or thrown away unknowingly).

A music notebook. The teacher usually suggests a specific notebook which will be used for keeping track of weekly lessons, writing assignments, practice records and other important information. It is advisable to buy a music notebook which is *large* enough so it won't be lost easily.

Pencils. Since most teachers give written assignments, supply your child with several pencils (pens, crayons or whatever the teacher requires). Put the pencils in your child's music case, and check periodically to make sure they are still there.

Music. Your teacher will assign the music necessary for lessons. Frequently, the music is selected and paid for by the teacher, and you are billed for it along with lesson fees. However, if the teacher requests that you purchase the music at a music store, be sure to purchase it *promptly* so your child will have it for practice right away. His progress will be hindered if new music is not obtained. In addition, it is embarrassing for a child to return to his lesson without the assigned music.

Cooperate with the teacher in the selection of music. Don't inform the teacher that your child can skip the basics and play "real music" (Bach, Chopin, etc.). It takes time for the beginner to absorb fundamentals. Learning to read music should be a step-by-step process in which the beginner advances at his own pace, building new musical facts on top of thoroughly learned old ones.

Don't be surprised if the music books assigned are not the same ones you had when you were taking lessons. You wouldn't expect your child to bring home the same math and science books you had when you were going to school. Many new piano teaching series have been published fairly recently. Included in most new series are basic course books, theory books, technic books and supplementary books. These playing and writing materials are designed to teach beginners basic information which should be learned gradually for thorough comprehension. If your child *understands* what he is doing, he will enjoy lessons and be successful. Therefore, trust your teacher in the selection of materials.

CHECKLIST

What materials will be needed?

- *a music case*
- *a music notebook*
- *pencils*
- *music*

Will classical or popular music be assigned?

Generally speaking, the teacher's main goal is to teach the beginner to read music. The music used for this purpose must be easy enough for the beginner to comprehend. Usually the method books assigned contain a balance of original music and folk music (no arranged popular music). These types of music are used in order to develop reading skills. Classical music by the masters (Bach, Beethoven, Brahms, etc.) is generally too difficult for the beginner.

For most beginners even simplified arrangements of popular music are also too difficult. However, a selection of original rock- and pop-type pieces is now available on an elementary level, and, unless totally adverse to popular music of any type, most teachers now combine lighter music along with a basic reading approach for the beginner.

CHECKLIST

Will classical or popular music be assigned?

• *original classical and popular music are generally too difficult for the beginner*

Should my child have music theory instruction?

Theory instruction is given to beginners to provide in-depth in-

formation about the component parts of music (notes, rests, intervals, chords, music terms, etc.). Harmonizing melodies, learning to transpose, and creating original music is often included in a theory program. Working on these various parts of music aids the student in understanding *how* music is made. Therefore, it is a significant help to have theoretical aspects taught along with learning to play the piano. Some teachers include theory instruction in the private lesson, others offer a separate theory class. Check with your teacher to make sure theory lessons are included in some manner.

CHECKLIST

Should my child have music theory instruction?

• *theory knowledge is essential to understanding music*

How will my child learn to count time?

This subject is included here because various systems of counting are introduced in newer method books. Your child may be using a system which is unfamiliar to you, and you need to have some knowledge of these systems so you can help your child learn to count time.

Music uses notes of different values. If you are unfamiliar with these, here is a table of note and rest values used by beginners.

NOTES		RESTS	
Whole	o	Whole	▬
Half	♩	Half	▬
Quarter	♩	Quarter	⸞
Eighth	♪	Eighth	ⸯ
Two Eighths	♫	(equals ⸞)	

Among beginning method books presently published, there are four different counting systems used:

1. *number counting*

   4 counts per measure
   4 kind of note receiving 1 count

   Example:

   Manner of counting: 1   2   3   4   1 2 3 4   1   2 and 3 4   1   2   3   4

2. *modified number counting*

   Example:

   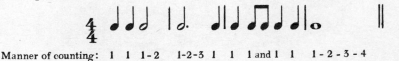

   Manner of counting: 1   1   1 - 2   1-2-3 1   1   1 and 1   1   1 - 2 - 3 - 4

3. *note name counting*

   Example:

   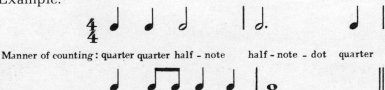

   Manner of counting : quarter quarter half - note   half - note - dot   quarter

   quarter two eighths quarter quarter   whole-note-hold - it

4. *Hungarian (or European) counting system*

Example:

Check your child's method book to see which counting system is used. By understanding these four counting systems you will be able to help your child count time.

CHECKLIST

How will my child learn to count time?

- *your child probably will learn one of four counting systems; familiarize yourself with these*

Should a metronome be used?

A metronome is a mechanical device for establishing the tempo of a piece. It is useful during practice sessions to check a steady beat. However, students should learn to "feel" the beat; the metronome should not be used as a crutch for this purpose.

Unless required by your teacher, first-year students do not need a metronome. It can be beneficially used from the second year on. The metronome helps students control tempo during practice. The student's idea of slow may be different from the teacher's. Therefore, if the teacher requires a metronome, cooperate and purchase one.

There are various types of metronomes: electric, transistor and wind-up models. Check with your teacher or personnel in a music store for suggestions.

CHECKLIST

Should a metronome be used?

• *the metronome generally is used later in music study*

Should my child memorize his music?

When playing for relatives and friends, in recitals, auditions or contests, it is advisable to play from memory. A child should not have to drag the music with him to be able to play a piece. However, not all the music studied should be memorized. Much of what is assigned is designed to improve music reading. Therefore, only special pieces need to be memorized (sheet music solos, for example).

CHECKLIST

Should my child memorize his music?

• *advisable when playing for an audience*

FIVE

PRACTICE SUGGESTIONS

Learning any new skill such as typing, a foreign language, or a sport, requires practice; the same is true for learning to play the piano. As a parent you can play a significant role in helping your child over the hurdles of practice.

How much should my child practice?

This question is usually the first one asked. For help in answering it, ask your child's teacher to recommend a certain length of time according to his age and grade. Probably the teacher will recommend a practice schedule which begins with a short amount of time and increases as your child's attention span increases.

Here is a general practice guide:

      15 minutes a day for the first month
      20 minutes a day for the next two months
      30 minutes a day for the remainder of the first year

More practice time will be required in succeeding years, depending on the child's interests and responsibilities in school and at home.

It will help your teacher if you encourage your child to write his practice time down in a music notebook. It is important for the teacher to know your child's practice record, because sometimes even though a great deal of practice time was spent, very little was accomplished. Likewise, a child may have used very little practice time to produce good results. By comparing the practice time with the results, your teacher can help accordingly.

Regarding practice time, it is not necessarily quantity that counts, but *quality*. Therefore, fifteen or twenty minutes of daily concentrated practice usually results in steady progress for the beginner.

CHECKLIST

How much should my child practice?

• *short periods at the beginning; longer as lessons progress*

When and how often should my child practice?

A child will respond more readily to his practice time if he has a *regular* time set aside each day. The scheduling of practice time should be given careful consideration to avoid conflicts with favorite TV programs, play periods, homework and fathers who insist on "peace and quiet."

If your child's attention span is short, use two short practice sessions: perhaps one before school, and one in the afternoon or evening. If your child arises early, the time before school is especially useful for practice, because there is no conflict from TV, play and scheduled activities.

Whether your child needs two short practice periods or one regular-length practice period, establish a *routine* which will be-

come a daily habit. You will be surprised to find that your child will come to think of his practice time as a normal part of the day, like meals, school, play and bedtime.

Daily practice is recommended because practice should not be crammed before the lesson. Time is needed to assimilate the week's lesson which can be learned best by spacing out practicing time during the week.

Be careful how you approach the practice time. Use gentle persuasion rather than brute force to get your child to the piano bench. Don't tell your child to "get in there and practice or you'll be punished and have to give up TV for a week." Rather, encourage your child to practice. Tell him you enjoy hearing him play, that he has done a great job so far this week, and that you are eager to hear what he can accomplish each day. Be quick to praise what he has done in practice sessions and slow to criticize. Also, be a bit flexible with a daily routine. If a conflict comes up during the regular practice time, adjust to another time to avoid antagonism and hostility from your child.

Your child may have difficulty practicing on the day of the lesson. If there is time before the lesson, a brief practice session is useful and helps bring the materials studied during the week into focus. If your child goes directly from school to his lesson, the only opportunity for practice prior to the lesson will be the morning period before school.

After the lesson, practicing is optional. Some children are eager to try new pieces assigned, others prefer to wait until the next day to resume the practice schedule.

What about missed practice periods due to unavoidable conflicts, such as doctor's or dentist's appointments, relatives or friends visiting, special trips, etc.? Conflicts such as these will occur; therefore, a little longer time can be given to succeeding practice sessions, and more time on the weekends can be utilized. Generally, aim for a six-day practice week; then, if a day is lost because of a conflict, a five-day practice week will suffice (for that week).

CHECKLIST

When and how often should my child practice?

- *establish a regular time(s) daily*
- *aim for a six-day practice week*

Should I help my child practice?

In the beginning nearly every child needs help between lessons. A guiding hand at home will be very helpful for your child and will please a grateful teacher. The language your child is learning is one totally unfamiliar and abstract to him—note and rest names, counting time, clef signs, key signatures, interval names, chord names, expression marks and Italian words. This is quite a big order for a youngster to learn on his own.

Your first valuable assistance should be to *organize* the practice session. In the beginning help your child read his assignment carefully to see what is expected of him for the week. By understanding the assignment, your child can use his time wisely instead of blindly plunging in. If written work is assigned, make sure your child has a supply of pencils handy, and check over the work to see that it has been done. Make sure *all* the assigned material is covered.

Try to keep all materials in a music case when your child is not practicing. Otherwise you may have to help your child gather his music together. Children have a way of scattering things, so that the assignment book is in the kitchen, the pencils are in the bedroom, some music is in the den, and some music has fallen behind the piano! Make sure *all* materials are in one place before your child starts to practice to avoid using up "practice time" for a room-to-room search.

When your child is practicing, try to keep him free from interruptions (dogs and cats, brothers and sisters, stereo or TV noise, etc.). Make sure his place of practice is quiet and well lit—a place which is generally conducive to concentration.

It is very important initially to develop good habits at the piano. Check with your teacher regarding height at the keyboard, posture and hand position. If you don't have an adjustable piano chair or stool at home, it may be necessary to raise your child up to the proper height at the keyboard with telephone books or cushions. Your teacher can give you good advice in this regard.

It is helpful for the beginner if the parent is nearby during practice sessions. If your child willingly accepts help, you can tactfully

assist him in making sure he understands the directions in his music book, helping him with notes, counting time, etc., and encouraging him to "try it once again."

If for some reason you cannot be in the room for any or all of the practice time (perhaps you are not at home, too busy, or your presence in the room creates problems), set aside several times during the week to hear your child's lesson. Your child will be eager to show you what he has accomplished, and you can bolster and encourage him by such phrases as: "It sounds beautiful"; "I love to hear you play"; or, "I'm so pleased how well you have done this week." Positive remarks will give your child confidence, which is what will be needed when he goes to his lesson where perhaps he will be told that his efforts were less than spectacular. Patience, persistence, enthusiasm and encouragement on your part will add fuel to the fire to kindle your child's musical interest.

CHECKLIST

Should I help my child practice?

- *help organize practice sessions*
- *keep practice sessions free from interruptions*
- *listen periodically to your child's lesson*

What if I don't know anything about music?

If you're a musical novice, take heart. You don't need to be a skilled musician to help your child practice, at least in the beginning stages. What is mainly needed from you is an interest in your child's accomplishments. A conscientious effort on your part to organize your child's practice time, make sure the assignment is completed and give encouragement at home may be more important incentives than those of a musically knowledgeable parent who nags at home for absolute perfection and injects musical views contrary to those of the teacher.

By helping your child practice from the beginning, you will learn basic music information which is easy to comprehend, even if you know nothing about music. In the beginning some standard folk song arrangements probably will be included among your child's pieces. If so, you should have no trouble helping in these practice sessions. Encourage your child to sing while practicing. You will be able to tell if the tune and rhythm are more or less correct. (Singing will help develop your child's "musical ear.") However, for more detailed aspects of music, you may need some help. Therefore, as an aid for parents without music knowledge, the music facts in Appendix A (see page 57) provide assistance.

Many parents become interested in taking lessons themselves through helping their children practice. This is an enjoyable hobby which gives a great deal of satisfaction and fulfillment. It's never too late to start. You might even surprise yourself!

CHECKLIST

What if I don't know anything about music?

- *show interest in your child's accomplishments*
- *help your child with familiar tunes*
- *acquaint yourself with basic music facts*

Should I reward my child for practicing?

You probably will want your child to take lessons for several years in order to give him an adequate music background. Although

you view practice now as time well spent which will result in good later, your child may not share your long-range view. He may see practicing as a daily task which cuts into his play time. He might not like having to assume responsibility for practicing which requires self-discipline. He may feel isolated and lonely during practice sessions. So in a sense, at this stage in his life, he is doing you a favor by practicing. For a favor, there should be a reward.

You can reward your child by showing appreciation for his music study in many ways. Praise him by telling him how proud you are of his accomplishments. Reward him with a trip to the zoo, a picnic outing, having a friend spend the night, or by giving him some other type of lessons (swimming, tennis, ballet, etc.) which he requests. You can also reward him by including his practice as part of his duties toward his weekly allowance. However you reward your child, do it in a way that lets him know that you *care* about his musical accomplishments, and that you appreciate his efforts. Bess Myerson states it aptly: "The greatest reward for a child . . . is the realization that the music is bringing pleasure, openly expressed, to the parents and to the teacher. A bravo or two never hurt anybody."[9]

CHECKLIST

Should I reward my child for practicing?

- *let your child know that you care about his musical accomplishments*
- *reward your child for his efforts in some concrete way*

---

[9]Bess Myerson, "My Mother, My Piano—And Me." Reprinted courtesy of *Redbook Magazine*, June 1974 issue.

SIX

RECITALS, CONTESTS, FESTIVALS AND AUDITIONS

Before discussing various aspects of recitals, contests, festivals and auditions, each should be defined.

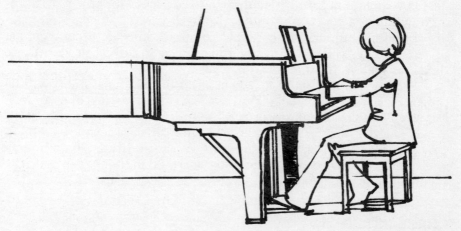

A *recital* is a concert given by a teacher's students. The students play in turn one or more pieces (solos, duets or two-piano selections).

A *contest* is a competition among several teachers' students for such prizes as cash, plaques, statues or ribbons. Winners are determined by a judge (or judges).

A *festival* or *audition* usually is an event in which a rating is given to each student by a judge (or judges). Usually this event is held privately. However, the term "festival" (or "tournament") is sometimes used to mean a contest.

Should my child participate?

A child who participates in scheduled events has definite goals to work toward. The incentive of competition or an adjudication rating can stimulate and motivate a student. However, the teacher's decision whether or not a child should participate should be respected. Likewise, the child's decision whether or not to participate should be given serious consideration.

From participating in recitals the student will gain self-confidence by proving to himself that he can do reasonably well under pressure. He will receive recognition and congratulations from parents, relatives, friends and his teacher, and thereby gain self-esteem and have a feeling of accomplishment. He will gain performance experience which will help him in contests and auditions. He will experience fulfillment in sharing music with peers and family.

From participating in contests the student will learn how his work compares with others (although, practically speaking, winning is often dependent to some degree on luck). The possibility of winning provides an incentive to practice for the event. Usually there is an adjudication report listing the student's strengths and weaknesses which is helpful in evaluating progress. Hopefully, the student will gain a sportsman-like attitude toward contests. There can only be a few winners in a contest. Competition is an integral aspect of our society, and a youngster must learn to adjust gracefully to defeat as well as to success.

From participating in festivals or auditions the student will be judged on his own merits; he will not have the pressure of a contest. His strengths and weaknesses will be indicated on an adjudication sheet. The possibility of receiving a high rating (superior, excellent, etc.) provides an incentive to practice for the audition. He will have goals to work toward which can be objictified in the form of ratings, certificates or the promotion to higher "grades" or levels.

CHECKLIST

Should my child participate?

- *your child will gain self-confidence*
- *he will have a goal to work toward and incentive to practice*

Are there any drawbacks?

If the child is not prepared adequately he will struggle just to get through the performance. His lack of preparation will make him ill at ease, will undermine his self-confidence, and will put him in a tense, awkward situation. Lack of preparation is a major obstacle to a successful performance. Also, children or parents who insist on performing against the teacher's advice can cause themselves unnecessary grief.

Some children are upset to the extreme if they do not win a contest. They might claim that they are no good and want to quit lessons because they did not win. Perhaps this type of child would be better off playing in an audition where he will be judged on his own merits rather than playing in a contest where winning is "everything" to him.

Finally, parents must be cautioned against "put-downs," either publicly or privately. Avoid telling your teacher after the recital in front of your child: "Mary played so well at home, it's too bad she didn't do her best tonight." Or later at home: "Mary, your performance really embarrassed me because it was so poor." Statements such as these can damage a child's self-confidence and can humiliate him unnecessarily. You must accept the fact that there is a degree of pressure in any performance, and your child may not always do his best. Therefore, offer praise and support wherever you can and omit cutting remarks.

CHECKLIST

Are there any drawbacks?

• *insufficient practicing may cause public embarrassment*

How can I help my child be prepared?

Encourage your child to practice *regularly.* The recital or contest piece cannot be "crammed" the night before the event. Systematic practice will give your child the self-confidence he needs to face a performance.

There is quite a difference between practicing and performing. A child may stop several times during a practice session for correction, but in a performance the piece must be played straight through. Therefore, have your child play the piece for you about two weeks before the scheduled event. You can tell if the piece is memorized securely, if the rhythm is correct, and if there is general continuity and self-assurance in the performance. If all is not well, there will be time to correct mistakes. If you have a tape recorder at home, have your child record his performance. When he hears himself in playback he can readily tell if his performance has continuity, correct rhythm, etc. Sometimes a child does not realize he is doing something incorrectly. Hearing his performance objectively makes him aware of faults and points out the areas in which he needs to improve.

Once a child is well prepared, he needs practice playing under pressure. Therefore, have him play for the family or for friends and relatives as often as possible. "Playing for visitors in the home is valuable in developing poise and self-assurance and should be tactfully encouraged by the parents when such opportunities present themselves."[10] However, if you do ask your young musician to play for friends or the family, be certain that the audience listens quietly and attentively until he is through. Talking or moving about during a performance is a definite put down. Also, avoid caustic remarks about the performance.

Prior to the performance create an aura of calmness (even if you're not!). Don't ask your child: "Aren't you nervous? I am!" Last minute jitters can easily undermine good preparation. Let your child settle down and think about the music. Avoid hovering over him like a hummingbird looking for a place to land.

Finally, a closing remark about performances: do your best to be present when your child performs. A recital is somewhat of a social event; your presence makes it a pleasant family outing and lends support to your child. By being there, you can give your child the appreciation he deserves.

CHECKLIST

How can I help my child be prepared?

- *encourage regular practice*
- *listen to your child play*

---

[10] Edmund W. Case, *Teacher, Parent, and Pupil* (Miami: Author, 1949). p. 105.

APPENDICES

APPENDIX A

Brief Outline of Musical Facts

1. THE PIANO KEYBOARD

The *white keys* on the keyboard are arranged in a recurring pattern of seven alphabet letters: A B C D E F G.

The *black keys* are grouped in sets of twos and threes. The black keys are called *sharps* or *flats*. The nearest key up to the right is called a sharp (♯). The nearest key down to the left is called a flat (♭).

SHARPS

FLATS

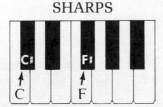
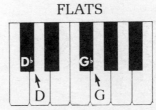

Keys on the piano which sound the same but look different in print are called *enharmonic*, such as C♯-D♭, E♯-F, C♭-B. (An English equivalent is *to, too, two.*)

2. THE STAFF

Music notation is written on a *staff* which has five lines and four spaces.

5 LINES

4 SPACES

The staff may be extended by adding short lines below or above it. These added lines are called *leger lines* (sometimes spelled ledger).

3. BAR LINES

Bar lines divide the staff into *measures*. A *double bar* indicates the end of a piece.

4. CLEF SIGNS

A *clef* (from the Latin, *clavis* meaning key) is placed at the beginning of each staff. The clef fixes the position of one letter (or pitch) as a point of reference for all other letters (pitches) on the staff.

Piano music uses two clef signs. The *treble clef* (or G *clef*) is centered upon the second line of the staff. The *bass clef* (or F *clef*) is centered upon the fourth line of the staff.

5. THE GRAND STAFF

Piano music is written on two staffs (or staves): the *treble staff* and the *bass staff*. High tones are written on the treble staff, low tones on the bass staff. The treble and bass staffs are joined by a *brace* and a *bar line* to form the *Grand Staff*.

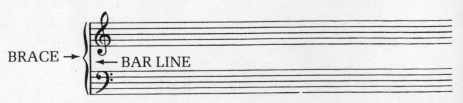

6. NOTES AND RESTS

Notes are written on the staff. Notes indicate both pitch and duration. Each note has an equivalent *rest*. Rests indicate measured silence.

NOTES		RESTS	
Whole	o	Whole	▬
Half	♩	Half	▬
Quarter	♩	Quarter	𝄽
Eighth	♪	Eighth	𝄾
Sixteenth	♫	Sixteenth	𝄿

7. NOTATION

Notes are written on *lines* and in *spaces* on the staff.

LINE NOTE ━o━   SPACE NOTE ═o═

Each note on the staff is to be played in a specific place on the keyboard. Notes below or above the staff are written on leger lines and spaces.

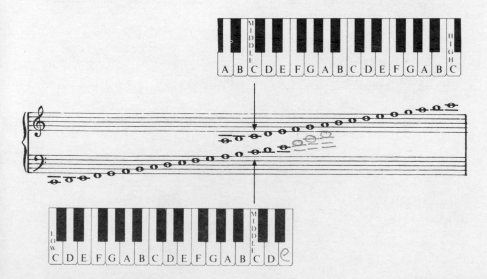

Notes are altered (raised or lowered) by *accidental* signs. The most frequently used accidental signs are the sharp (♯), flat (♭) and natural (♮) signs. These signs are printed before the note. The effect of the accidental lasts for a *whole* measure.

SHARP: Play the nearest key up to the right, either black or white.

FLAT: Play the nearest key down to the left, either black or white.

NATURAL: A natural cancels other accidentals. Play a "natural" white key.

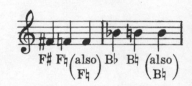

8. TIME SIGNATURES

A *time signature* (or *meter signature*) has two numbers. The upper number indicates the number of beats (or counts) in a measure. The lower number indicates what kind of note receives one beat (or count).

Some frequently used time signatures are $\frac{2}{4}, \frac{3}{4}, \frac{4}{4}, \frac{2}{2}, \frac{6}{8}$.

A sign called *common time* (**C**) is often used in place of $\frac{4}{4}$.

$$\mathbf{C} = \frac{4}{4}$$

A sign called *alla breve*, or "cut time" (**¢**) is often used in place of $\frac{2}{2}$

$$\mathbf{\mathcal{C}} = \frac{2}{2}$$

9. RHYTHMIC NOTATION*

Notes receive different beats (or counts) dependent on the time signature. Two frequently used types of rhythm patterns are shown as examples.

TABLE A

$\frac{2}{4}$, $\frac{3}{4}$, $\frac{4}{4}$ TIME SIGNATURES		
Notes	Beats	Rhythm Patterns
𝅝	4	𝅝
𝅗𝅥.	3 (a dot increases the value of a note by one half)	𝅗𝅥. ♩
𝅗𝅥	2	𝅗𝅥 𝅗𝅥
♩	1	♩ ♩ ♩ ♩
♪	½	[eighth notes pattern]
♬	¼	[sixteenth notes pattern]

TABLE B

$\frac{3}{8}$, $\frac{6}{8}$, $\frac{9}{8}$ TIME SIGNATURES		
Notes	Beats	Rhythm Patterns
𝅗𝅥.	6	𝅗𝅥.
♩.	3	♩. ♩.
♩	2	♩ ♪ ♩ ♪
♪	1	[eighth notes pattern]
♬	½	[sixteenth notes pattern]

*See page 41 for various ways of counting rhythm in children's method books.

An exception to the rhythm in TABLE A is the *triplet*:  . A triplet is an irregular pattern of three notes played in the time of two.

This rhythm pattern is used frequently in $\frac{2}{4}$, $\frac{3}{4}$ and $\frac{4}{4}$ time.

10. INTERVALS

Intervals are used to make melodies. An interval is the distance in pitch between two tones (notes).

Intervals may be either *melodic* (notes played one-at-a-time)

or *harmonic* (notes played together).

INTERVALS THROUGH THE OCTAVE

2nd 3rd 4th 5th 6th 7th 8th (octave)

An accidental changes the sound of the interval, but not its number name. Thus, C-G, C-G♭, C-G♯ are all fifths, even though they sound different. Their names are *perfect, diminished* and *augmented*, respectively.

11. HALF STEPS AND WHOLE STEPS

Tonal relationships may be measured by interval terminology; some tonal relationships may also be measured by *half step* and *whole step* terminology. On the piano these may be described as:

HALF STEP: from one key to the nearest key with *no key in between.*

WHOLE STEP: from one key to a neighbor key with *one key in between.*

12. SCALES

The word *scale* comes from the Latin word *scala*, meaning ladder. A scale has an arrangement of tones in a pattern (like steps on a ladder). Scale tones are used to make compositions. Although many scales are used in music, two types of scales are used most frequently: *Major scales* and *minor scales*.

Major scales have a pattern of whole and half steps.

MAJOR SCALE: half steps between 3-4 and 7-8
                                            (all others are whole steps)

Scale tones: 1   2   3   4   5   6   7   8

Unlike the Major scale which has only one form, the minor scale has three forms: *natural, harmonic* and *melodic.*

NATURAL MINOR SCALE: half steps between 2-3 and 5-6

Scale tones: 1   2   3   4   5   6   7   8

HARMONIC MINOR SCALE: half steps between 2-3, 5-6
                          and 7-8

Scale tones: 1   2   3   4   5   6   7   8

Scale tones: 1 2 3 4 5 6 7 8   8 7 6 5 4 3 2 1

MELODIC MINOR SCALE: half steps between 2-3 and 7-8
                            ascending;
                            half steps between 6-5 and 5-2
                            descending

Scale tones: 1 2 3 4 5 6 7 8   8 7 6 5 4 3 2 1

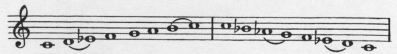

Scale tones (*steps* or *degrees* of the scale) are given the following names:

1. Tonic (or *key note*)
2. Supertonic
3. Mediant
4. Subdominant
5. Dominant
6. Submediant
7. Leading Tone

13. KEY SIGNATURES

A *key signature* is a group of sharps or flats at the beginning of each staff. Rather than writing every sharp or flat as an accidental throughout a piece (as in the scales above), the key signature is used for convenience. The key signature indicates two things:

1. The notes to be sharped or flatted throughout the entire piece.
2. The main key (tonic key) of the piece.

Sharps and flats are always written in the same order on the staff.

The order of sharps is: F C G D A E B
The order of flats is: B E A D G C F

Note: the sequence of flats is the same as the sharps, but in *reverse*.

The rules for naming Major *sharp* key signatures are:

1. Look at the last sharp to the right:
2. Go *up* to the next letter in the musical alphabet (one half step), this is the name of the Major key.

D MAJOR

The rules for naming Major *flat* key signatures are:

1. Look at the next-to-the-last flat:
2. The name of this letter is the name of the Major key.

B♭ MAJOR

3. *Exceptions:*

Key of F
(one flat only)

Key of C
(no sharps or flats)

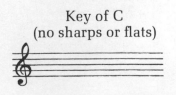

Every key signature applies to two keys, both Major and minor, such as G Major and E minor (both have one sharp). The following table identifies all Major and minor key signatures.

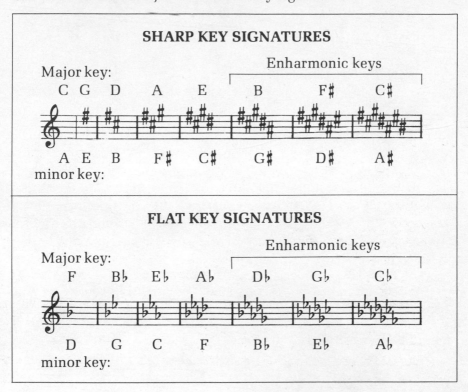

14. CHORDS

A *chord* is a combination of simultaneously-sounding tones. Chords provide harmony in music. Chords are "spelled" from the lowest tone upwards (thus, C E G, not G E C). Chords are formed from musical alphabet skips (C E G, C E G B, C E G B D) which are a third apart.

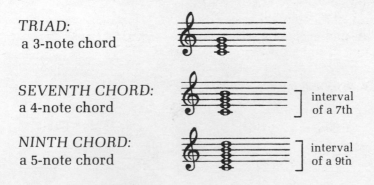

TRIAD:
a 3-note chord

SEVENTH CHORD:
a 4-note chord
interval of a 7th

NINTH CHORD:
a 5-note chord
interval of a 9th

There are four kinds of triads, classified according to the nature of the intervals formed between the root (lowest note of the chord) and the other two tones.

MAJOR TRIAD: major 3rd, perfect 5th

MINOR TRIAD: minor 3rd, perfect 5th

AUGMENTED TRIAD: major 3rd, augmented 5th

DIMINISHED TRIAD: minor 3rd, diminished 5th

A chord can be built on any scale tone. The chord gets its name from its root.

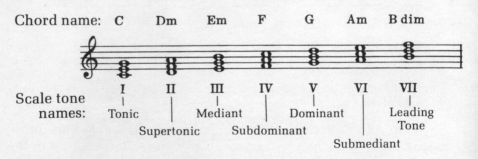

Chord name: C   Dm   Em   F   G   Am   B dim

Scale tone names: I Tonic   II Supertonic   III Mediant   IV Subdominant   V Dominant   VI Submediant   VII Leading Tone

Any chord may be *inverted* (rearranged). A triad is inverted by moving the root note to the top or middle.

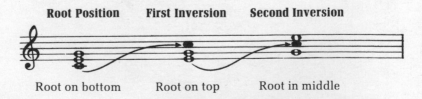

Root Position   First Inversion   Second Inversion

Root on bottom   Root on top   Root in middle

APPENDIX B

Brief Dictionary of Musical Terms

TEMPO   Indicates rate of speed

Largo—broadly, very slowly
Lento—slowly
Adagio—slowly, leisurely
Andante—a walking pace, flowing
Andantino—slightly faster than andante
Moderato—moderately
Allegretto—quickly, but not as fast as allegro
Allegro—at a quick pace, lively
Vivace or Vivo—lively
Presto—very fast
Prestissimo—faster than presto

Changing Tempos

Accelerando (*accel.*) to become faster
A tempo—resume original tempo
Mosso—motion
Moto—motion; (*con moto*) with motion, or quicker
Rallentando (*rall.*) gradually slowing in speed
Ritardando (*rit.*) becoming slower
Ritenuto (*riten.*) immediate slowing

DYNAMICS   Pertaining to the volume of sound.

Pianissimo (*pp*) very soft
Piano (*p*) soft
Mezzo piano (*mp*) moderately soft
Mezzo forte (*mf*) moderately loud
Forte (*f*) loud
Fortissimo (*ff*) very loud
Sforzando (*sfz*) strong accent

Changing Dynamics

Crescendo (*cresc.*) growing louder ————————
Descrescendo (*descresc.*) growing softer ————————
Diminuendo (*dim., dimin.*) growing softer

STYLE   The character of mood of the composition.

Animato—animated, with spirit
Brio—vigor, spirit
Cantabile—singing
Dolce—sweetly
Expressivo (*espress.*) with expression, feeling
Giocoso—humorously
Grazioso—gracefully
Legato (*leg.*) smoothly connected tones
Maestoso—majestically
Marcia—as a march
Portamento—slightly disconnected tones
Scherzando—playfully
Sostenuto—sustained
Staccato (*stacc.*) disconnected tones
Tenuto (*ten.*) held note
Tranquillo—calm, quiet, tranquil

MISCELLANEOUS TERMS

Coda—ending
Con—with
D. C. (*Da Capo*) go to the beginning
D. C. al Fine—repeat from the beginning to the end (Fine)
D. S. (*Dal Segno*) the sign 𝄋
D. S. al Fine—repeat from the sign to the end (Fine)
Fermata—pause, or hold the note 𝄐
Fine—the end
Loco—in normal location or pitch register
Meno—less
Molto—much
Non—not
Piu—more
Poco—a little
Poco a poco—little by little, gradually
Sempre—always
Simile—in a similar way
Troppo—too much

NOTES AND RESTS

𝅝   whole note

𝅗𝅥   half note

♩   quarter note

♪   eighth note

♪ sixteenth note

♬ thirty-second note

♪ grace note—to be played quickly

arpeggiated, or rolled chord

whole rest   eighth rest

half rest   sixteenth rest

quarter rest   thirty-second rest

SIGNS

♯ sharp   ✗ double sharp

♭ flat   ♭♭ double flat

♮ natural   *8va* octave

⌢ fermata   portamento

staccato   triplet

1.   2.   first and second endings

stress, accent, strong accent

C (*common time*) 4 beats to the measure (4/4)

₵ (*alla breve*) 2 strong beats to the measure (2/2)

repeat sign

tied notes

slurred notes

Ped., P, ⌐___⌐   ∧_∧ _ pedal indications

APPENDIX C

Brief Reference Listing

MUSIC

Children's Music Books

Davis, Marilyn K., and Arnold Broido. *Music Dictionary*. Garden City, N.Y.: Doubleday, 1968.

Greene, Carla. *Let's Learn about the Orchestra*. Irvington-on-Hudson, N.Y.: Harvey House, 1967.

Wechsberg, Joseph. *The Pantheon Story of Music for Young People*. New York: Pantheon Books, 1968.

Winn, Marie, ed. *The Fireside Book of Children's Songs*, arranged by Allan Miller, New York: Simon and Schuster, Inc., 1966.

Histories

Britten, Benjamin, and Imogen Holst. *The Wonderful World of Music*. Garden City, N.Y.: Doubleday, 1968. Presents a concise history of music, musicians, and instruments in easy to read language. Contains an excellent glossary of terms for the layman.

Hindley, Geoffrey, ed. *The Larousse Encyclopedia of Music*. New York: The World Publishing Co., 1971. A beautifully illustrated history of music. Contains an excellent glossary of technical terms and musical instruments.

Introductory Books

Bernstein, Leonard. *The Joy of Music*. New York: Simon & Schuster, Inc., 1959.

Copland, Aaron. *What to Listen for in Music*, Revised Edition. New York: McGraw-Hill Book Co., Inc., 1957.

Gillespie, John. *The Musical Experience*, Second Edition. Belmont, California: Wadsworth Publishing Co., 1972.

Machlis, Joseph. *The Enjoyment of Music*, Third Edition/shorter. New York: W. W. Norton & Co., Inc., 1970.

Musical Ability

Fisher, Renee B. *Musical Prodigies: Masters at an Early Age.* New York: Association Press, 1973.

Pianists

Schoenberg, Harold C. *Great Pianists From Mozart to the Present.* New York: Simon & Schuster, Inc., 1963.

Piano Care

Schmeckel, Carl D. *The Piano Owners Guide.* Sheboygan, Wis.: Apex Piano Publishing, 1971.

PSYCHOLOGY

Brumbaugh, Florence N., and Bernard Roshco. *Your Gifted Child.* New York: Collier Books, 1962. Offers constructive advice about how to give your child extra intellectual help. Explains what gifted children are like.

Dodson, Dr. Fitzhugh. *How to Parent.* New York: Signet/The New American Library, Inc., 1970. A specialized study of children from infancy through preschool age. Contains extensive appendices dealing with selecting good books, educational toys, play equipment, and records for children.

Ginott, Dr. Haim G. *Between Parent and Child.* New York: The Macmillan Co., 1965. Shows parents the difference between destructive and constructive conversations with children. Especially helpful is the advice on "Music Lessons," pages 82-85.

Gordon, Dr. Thomas. *P.E.T. Parent Effectiveness Training.* New York: Peter H. Wyden, Inc., 1970. Offers excellent advice in dealing with parent-children problems. Contains a brief, but good, bibliography.

Harris, Dr. Thomas A. *I'm OK—You're OK.* New York: Avon Books, 1973. Offers lucid insights into relationships with others. Contains a great deal of practical advice for relationships between parents and children.